The Wrestling Cholitas of Bolivia

OTHER TITLES IN
THE COLLECTION

Girls Rock Indonesia
The Mermaids of Jamaica
The Amazing Students of Venezuela

Written by
CLAUDIA BELLANTE

Illustrated by
ANNA CARBONE

The Wrestling Cholitas of Bolivia

Crocodile Books, USA

An imprint of Interlink Publishing Group, Inc.

www.interlinkbooks.com

To Tina, my little wrestling cholita,
and Mirko, with whom I discovered Latin America
and all the stories about it.

Claudia

· · · ·

To Giovanni and Tito, always with me
in all my adventures.

Anna

First American edition published 2022 by
CROCODILE BOOKS
An imprint of Interlink Publishing Group, Inc.
46 Crosby Street, Northampton, Massachusetts 01060
www.interlinkbooks.com

Library of Congress Cataloging-in-Publication Data available
ISBN 978-1-62371-807-7 · hardback

Printed and bound in Korea on forest-friendly paper
10 9 8 7 6 5 4 3 2 1

FSC
www.fsc.org
MIX
Paper | Supporting
responsible forestry
FSC® C023083

Against All Odds was born out of the desire to tell our kids real stories of children living in distant places and facing unique situations.

The series talks about everyday gestures that in certain contexts can become important, even to the point of changing the course of events, defying prejudices and clichés, and redirecting our attention to often-overlooked problems.

All of the events described in these books really happened or are currently happening. Only the protagonists are the result of the poetic license; the author wanted to protect the identities of the minors involved in these stories.

In El Alto, Bolivia, the air is often thin and it's hard to breathe. Mountains embrace the city and, if you raise your hands, you can touch the clouds.

Many people who live in El Alto came from the countryside and speak an ancient indigenous language: Aymara.

Almost all the houses in El Alto are short and made of bricks, but an ingenious and flamboyant architect named Freddy Mamani recently started constructing buildings that are beautiful and colorful, with huge ballrooms and crystal chandeliers.

These palaces, worthy of kings and queens, have become world-famous and allow the inhabitants to feel proud of their city and their origins.

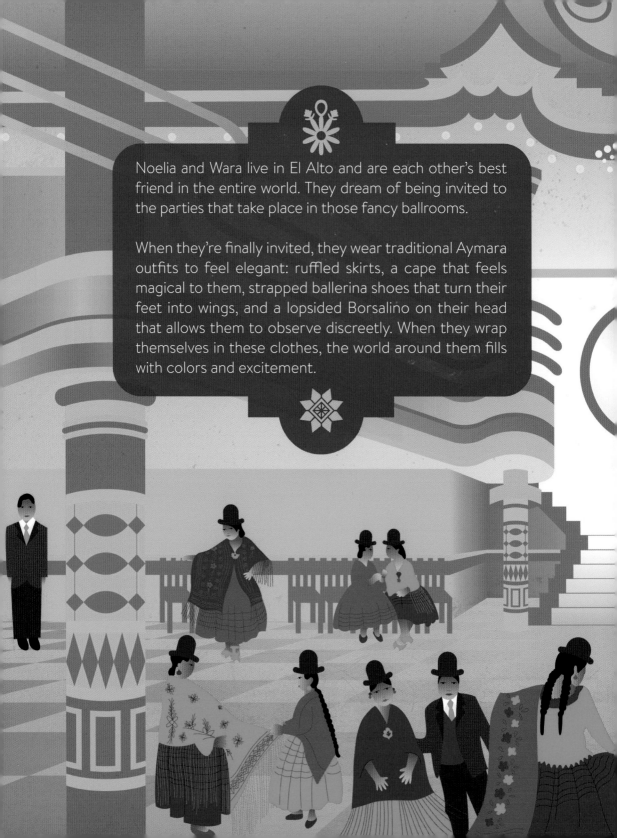

Noelia and Wara live in El Alto and are each other's best friend in the entire world. They dream of being invited to the parties that take place in those fancy ballrooms.

When they're finally invited, they wear traditional Aymara outfits to feel elegant: ruffled skirts, a cape that feels magical to them, strapped ballerina shoes that turn their feet into wings, and a lopsided Borsalino on their head that allows them to observe discreetly. When they wrap themselves in these clothes, the world around them fills with colors and excitement.

The girls and women in Bolivia who dress like this are called *cholitas*. In the past, cholitas were powerless and could only access the most humble jobs because they came from the countryside, didn't speak Spanish, and lacked formal education. Today, things have changed. They've become a symbol of Bolivian culture, which has encouraged respect and admiration for them.

Noelia's father is a bus driver. He drives around the streets of El Alto in the hell of smog and horns. Her mother has a small restaurant near the cable car stop, where she cooks rice, potatoes, and chicken in large quantities. Wara's father died, and her mother has a fruits-and-vegetables stall in the market that gives them just enough to live.

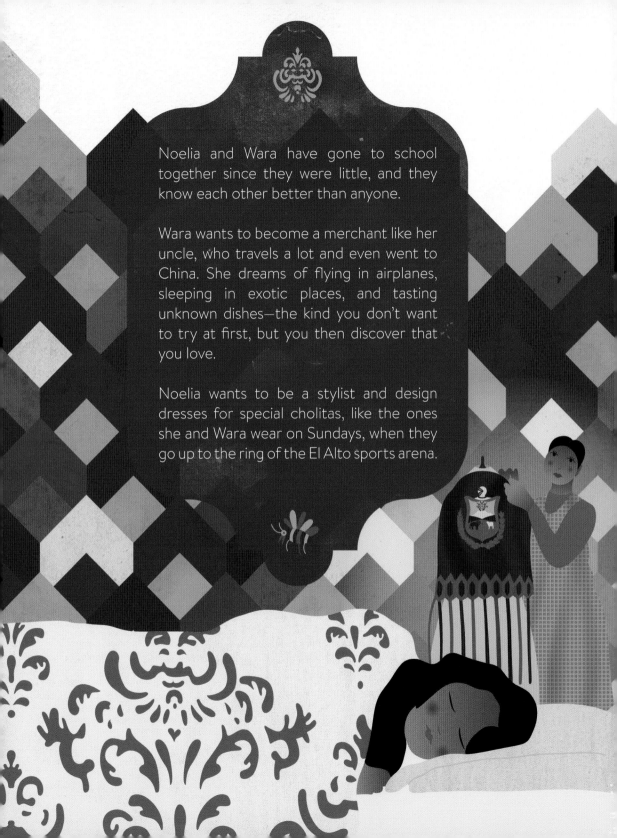

Noelia and Wara have gone to school together since they were little, and they know each other better than anyone.

Wara wants to become a merchant like her uncle, who travels a lot and even went to China. She dreams of flying in airplanes, sleeping in exotic places, and tasting unknown dishes—the kind you don't want to try at first, but you then discover that you love.

Noelia wants to be a stylist and design dresses for special cholitas, like the ones she and Wara wear on Sundays, when they go up to the ring of the El Alto sports arena.

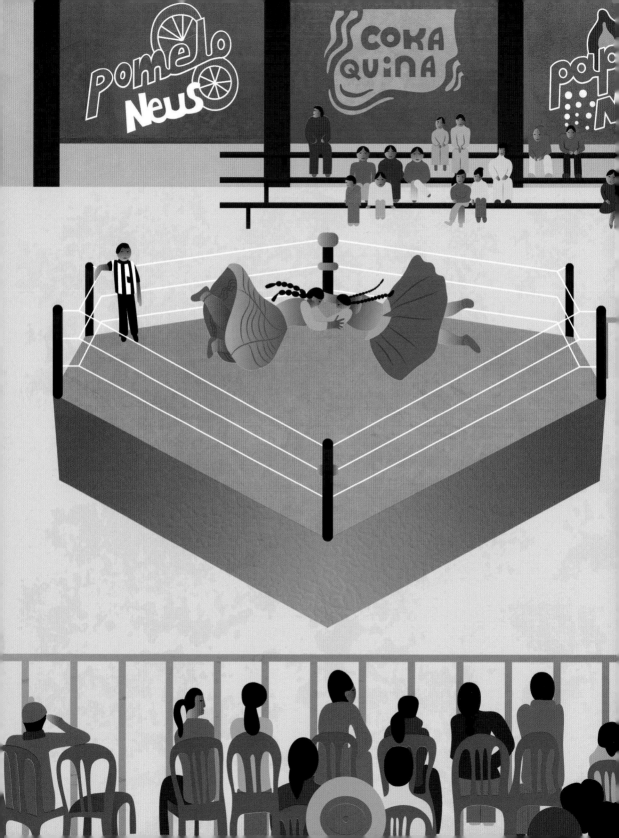

VISCACHANI

Noelia and Wara are fighting cholitas. On the weekends, they transform from diligent students into fearless warriors, participating in freestyle wrestling matches.

Some of their peers don't understand why they practice a sport that's considered "for boys," but they couldn't care less. They step into the ring and challenge their opponents with flying kicks and impeccable fists. Fortunately, the blows aren't real, just staged for the audience, although sometimes they really do get hurt.

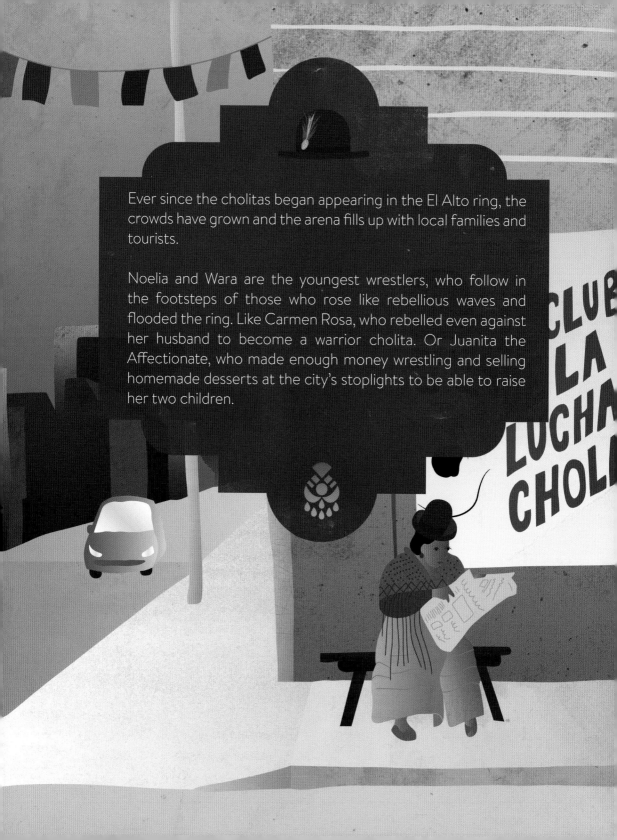

Ever since the cholitas began appearing in the El Alto ring, the crowds have grown and the arena fills up with local families and tourists.

Noelia and Wara are the youngest wrestlers, who follow in the footsteps of those who rose like rebellious waves and flooded the ring. Like Carmen Rosa, who rebelled even against her husband to become a warrior cholita. Or Juanita the Affectionate, who made enough money wrestling and selling homemade desserts at the city's stoplights to be able to raise her two children.

CLUB
LA
LUCHA
CHOL

DE EL INTERIOR DE LAS ANDES, ELLA CONQUISTÓ EL MUNDO

HOLITA LUCHADORA

HINCHIN

SI ERES UN HÉROE LOCAL PUEDES SER UN HÉROE GLOBAL

EL OJO DE IBEROAMÉRICA

KATH

La Hermos

The most famous cholitas often go on tour to neighboring countries, such as Peru and Argentina, and they have many admirers. Despite the fame and applause, being a luchadora in Bolivia is not easy, because you have to fight against those who believe a girl shouldn't wrestle.

"It's a boy thing," "You'll hurt yourself," "You'll never have a boyfriend if you continue this way," their parents say.

But the cholitas laugh and keep going.

When they go to school, Noelia and Wara wear normal clothes: jeans, sweatshirts, tennis shoes. But to wrestle, they each have their own style.

Noelia loves bright colors, and her skirts are usually bright yellow or pink. She never leaves without her shawl and has some very nice ones that she borrows from her mother, who always begs her not to mess them up too much. She fastens them with unusual and threatening-looking fashion-jewelry brooches shaped like fists or skulls so they won't fall off.

Wara, on the other hand, is the biggest fan of traditional Mexican wrestling masks.

Becoming a wrestling cholita takes time and sacrifice. On Tuesdays, there are workouts with weights, races, and other exercises; on Thursdays, practice in the ring; and on Saturdays, a dress rehearsal for the Sunday show. The other days, they rest, although there is always homework left to do.

Among the most spectacular moves that the cholitas are capable of are the pirouettes, which allow the audience to see the skirts' endless pleats that turn into magic circles, and the jumps from the ropes that make their long black braids slice the air like sharp knives.

Little by little, match after match, Noelia and Wara are becoming famous wrestling cholitas. Still, when the noise and the applause and the cheers cease, the warrior goddesses become two regular girls, worried about a math test or an argument with their parents.

But the glory is already attached to their dresses and tangled in their hair, which is evident in the way they fight small daily battles.

There are two types of wrestling cholitas: the "bad" ones, who become beasts in the ring, disregard the rules, and are mean even to their fans, and the "good" ones, who execute moves impeccably and affectionately make conversation with the audience.

Noelia and Wara are the "good" kind and therefore never wrestle against each other. They both love to do pirouettes in the air, jump until they almost touch the sky, and every time they nimbly dodge a hit, they turn to the cheering crowds with a grateful smile. They often win and sometimes lose, but it doesn't matter; they're there to have fun.

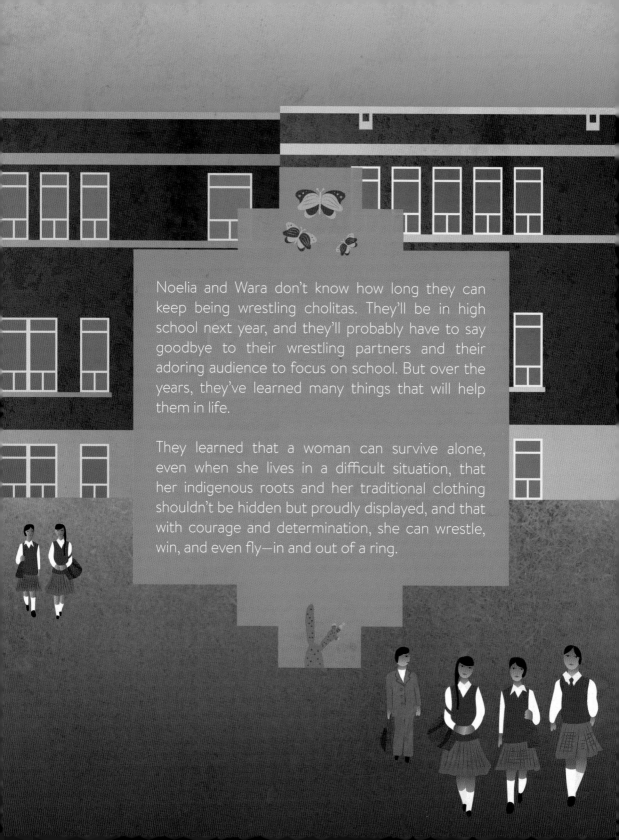

Noelia and Wara don't know how long they can keep being wrestling cholitas. They'll be in high school next year, and they'll probably have to say goodbye to their wrestling partners and their adoring audience to focus on school. But over the years, they've learned many things that will help them in life.

They learned that a woman can survive alone, even when she lives in a difficult situation, that her indigenous roots and her traditional clothing shouldn't be hidden but proudly displayed, and that with courage and determination, she can wrestle, win, and even fly—in and out of a ring.

AUTHOR'S NOTE

In recent years, I've traveled to El Alto several times. Its architecture, chaos, and especially the cholitas—women and girls who don their traditional clothes at every moment of the day and who have earned a place of power in Bolivian society—have always fascinated me.

I love their skirts, their Borsalino hats, their colors, their pride, and their playfulness. I know cholitas that practice all kinds of professions: guards, models, chefs, radio journalists, activists, and parliamentarians. However, I decided to tell the story of the wrestling cholitas, because it is surely the most unique aspect of their emancipation and because behind the spectacle lies a deep search for self-determination, great strength, and a unique desire to dismantle prejudice.

Claudia Bellante